Heartscapes

Larry L. Black

This book is dedicated to all those who have touched my life and my heart. To those who have encouraged me when I needed it, and who have taught me how to accept love and loss. To those who have stood by me through difficult times and still stand by my side today.

Contents

Whispers In the Wind

Whispers in the wind speak gently to my soul. Whispers, soft against my ears.

They speak of a world in turmoil, a world in pain. Peace tainted by the belief that the color of skin can be an excuse for fear; that fear can become the core of hate. They speak of the need of power by those who have the wealth to strip the world of the glue called humanity.

Whispers in the wind speak gently to my soul. Whispers, soft against my ears.

They speak of the ignorance of those who do not believe that a man can love a man, that a woman can love a woman, that the sex of either can change to become the person they are meant to be. They speak of the fear this love causes; the fear that can become the core of hate.

Whispers in the wind speak gently to my soul. Whispers, soft against my ears.

They speak of false truths and personal gains by those who, "we the people" have placed our trust in to make the world a better place. To make lives equal, and to understand that all lives matter. They speak of the inability of those we have chosen to dispel the fear; the fear that can become the core of hate.

Whispers in the wind speak gently to my soul. Whispers, soft against my ears.

They speak of the power within each of us to bring peace to a troubled world. Take the hand of a stranger. Have the courage to understand and learn about that which causes you fear. Let your voice be heard in a peaceful way. Take a stand for what is right. Do not let your fear become the core of hate.

Whispers in the wind. Soft against my ears.

Wishes In the Night

Midnight… the sky glitters – and I am overwhelmed
by the wonder of the night.

The stars sing as if orchestrated by the moon. Each
twinkle carries a chord of beauty that is music to
my soul. The night song touches my heart, filling
it with hope.

I wish upon the stars, that this divided land will
come together. I wish. I wish… that color and
gender and race will find peace as one.

I wish upon the stars… that sexual preference will
find acceptance and contentment in a world of
ignorance and fear.

I Wish. I wish… that lands ravaged by this angry
earth will receive the help to prosper and grow strong.

Wishes upon a star. Stars singing the wonder of the night, the
wonder of this earth.

I wish. I wish... among the beauty of the stars singing in the night.

Rain So Soft

Rain so soft,
Please wash away the pain.
Take away the heartbreak,
please make me whole again.

Take my fears, gently please,
and wash them all away.
I'm naked and afraid,
wishing for a better day

Wash away the doubt,
let it puddle at my feet.
Gentle rain, heal my heart.
Rain so soft, so sweet

Rain so soft,
please wash away the pain
Take away the heartbreak,
please make me whole again

Gently rain, drop by drop,
restore my faith in me.
Cleanse the hurt, cleanse the pain
and let my heart be free

Softly rain, wash my tears.
Let them fall and fade away.
Let them puddle at my feet.
Let me find new strength this day

Rain so soft,
please wash away the pain
Take away the heartbreak,
please make me whole again.

Just A Word

Alone.
Just a word, really.
Except at night.
Then it becomes
What you are.
It embraces you with
A sadness that can
Be suffocating

Alone.
Just a word.
Just a word until
The darkness comes.
The darkness, with the doubts
And the wonder of
Where dreams went.

Alone.
When you try to
Find the pieces of you.
Try to put them back
Together in the dark.
Try to put yourself together again.

Alone.
The time to find solace
In the memories of
Who you used to be.
The time to find the
Courage to become
That person again.

Alone.
When you try find the
Pieces of you.
Alone.
When you try to put
Yourself together again.

You Can Do This

As you begin this new journey
in your life, know that you have
the strength to see it through.

I know you have your doubts,
but you are stronger than you
think you are. You have the faith
and the will to succeed.

You were raised to know the value
of self, and the importance of clear
and positive thought. Only you can
make this happen. You can do this.

Please know that you are not alone.
I am with you on this journey. My
heart, my prayers, my love – these are
the things I give to you – these are
the things that you can draw upon when
the burden of this journey seems
more than you can bear.

Know that you have the strength
to see this through. Know that
you possess the will to succeed.
Know that you can make this
happen – and above all, know that
you are not on this journey alone.

Loving You

The coffee ring from your cup still stains the table.
I clean around it each day – afraid to clean away
the memory of you. I remember your morning smile,
how you would laugh at my attempt to flip the eggs in the pan
without breaking the yolk. I still talk to you some mornings.
Silly. I know. But it helps to get me through the day.

I hold your pillow close to me each night – just to get
the scent of you. I know your scent is gone, but I pretend.
Pretend that I can feel the warmth of you.
I snuggle close to the memory of you.
Silly. I know. But it helps to get me through the night.

I remember the songs that would make us dance. How you
would drag me to the dance floor. Me looking the fool while you moved
with such grace. And the movies. We would laugh and mimic,
and sometimes cry. And now… I dance alone, still looking the fool.
I don't laugh much anymore. But I cry. I cry alone.
Silly. I know. But it helps to get me through the pain.

And the day you were taken from this earth. That is perhaps the most special each year. The day I celebrate the joy of loving you. The day I celebrate the beauty you brought to this earth. The day that brings me comfort that came from loving you.

Silly. I know. But it helps me believe that one day, we will be together again.

Believe In Me

Believe in me, my friend.
Know that friendship is
not a word I use to describe
just someone I know.

Trust that I know the fears
within your heart. That I
have shared the worries that
burden your soul

Take heart in knowing
that if your tears should
need to fall – I will be
there to dry them away.

On those days that you
need a hug to make it
through the day – know
that my embrace will
be strong and true.

Believe in me, my friend.
You can place your trust
in me. Take my hand.
Feel safe in the warmth
of a kindred soul.

When you feel weak,
please find a strength
in me. Take my hand.
Share your dreams.
You have a friend in me.

Stay Safe My Dreams

I found my dreams today.
Withered and stale. Broken
pieces too fragile to hold onto.
Afraid that if I try too hard to believe
in them they will crumble into the
wind and drift away.

Stay safe my dreams, stay strong.

I gathered them with care and put
them in a safe place – a place known
only to me. Away from further
harm – for if they are lost, then I
will become the broken man I've tried
so hard not to be.

Stay safe my dreams, stay strong.

In time, I will gather them again. Piece
them together. Make them stronger.
Perhaps I will have the strength to
keep them whole, the strength to believe in
them again.

Stay safe my dreams. Stay strong.

Take My Hand

In those moments that you
feel alone, that it is you against
the world – take my hand.
Feel safe in knowing that
there is someone by your side

When you think that you
are not loved – take my hand.
Know that you are loved for the
person you are, and not the person
that people want you to be.

At those times when it is difficult
to take another step – take my hand.
Let me help lead you to the
place that will make you stronger, the
place that will help you grow.

When you are afraid of this place
called now – take my hand.
Know that there is a better
place waiting for you, but
that it will take your own
strength to get there.

When you need shelter – take my hand.
Take strength in knowing that
my door is always open.
Feel safe in the arms of
friendship and love.

Take my hand.
Be strong.
Be safe.
Be loved.

Take my hand.

Stop Hate Now

STOP THE
Indifference
Profiling
Ignorance
Prejudice
Fear

STOP THE HATE OF
Color
Uniform
Sexual Preference
Race
Religion

EMBRACE
Knowledge
Understanding
Acceptance
Joined Hands
Compassion

 Tonight

Tonight, I wonder how we
grew apart… how we let
the moments of time and distance
become the enemy of our love.

I wonder at what point you
decided our relationship was broken,
and why you couldn't see that ours
was a love worth saving.

Tonight, I wonder why you let
him in. I wonder how, in a time
of our loss, he could become the
love to replace mine, The one
to replace the years we shared.

I wonder how I can lose any more
of myself to you – why I still love
you – when I know your love is gone.
I wonder how my heart, so empty,
still has the strength to get me through
each day.

Tonight, I wonder how we grew apart.
I wonder how a heart so empty can
love so much. I wonder…
why you let him in.

Please, Remember My Love

I loved you more than I loved myself,
put your feelings above mine.
I wasn't quite whole without you by my side.
I became so much a part of you
that I lost the true sense of who I used to be.

It seems that wasn't enough.
You wanted more than I could offer.
You needed more than I could give.
A perfect world of physical and emotional
bliss untethered by the reality of life.
I ask that you please remember.
Please remember my love.

You feel the need to grow without me by your side.
The need to find the perfect love.
I'll be watching to make sure you find a
love without hurt, a love without pain.
A love without the things you've given me.
I ask that you please remember.
Please remember my love.

I wish for you a happiness that will be difficult to find.
A wish that you will find a love as strong as mine.
That you find that one person that you want to
grow old with by your side.
But most of all I wish that you remember.
Please remember my love.

Once Whole, Now Broken

Thinking of you, of us,
once whole - now broken.
I am afraid to face the pain.
Afraid that it will destroy me -
afraid that each beat of my
heart will remind me of you.

Afraid that each tear that falls
upon my face will wash away
my strength to face each day.
Each day filled with truths too
painful to bear. Each day leading
to a sleepless night filled with
a loneliness that chills my soul.

Thinking of you, of us,
once whole - now broken.
I am afraid to face the pain.
Afraid that the pieces of my
broken dreams will never quite
fit together again.
Afraid of the person I have
become in the wake of a
love once whole - now broken.

Afraid. Afraid of where I am
without you. Afraid of what the
pain and loneliness will bring.
Afraid of another day, leading
to another night, and the person
I have become…
Once whole - now broken.

I'm Here

I know you feel that life has
kicked you in the teeth.
That things will never be the same, and
that sadness is your new best friend.

It's okay to feel this way.
It's okay to be sad, but please know one thing.
You are not alone.
I'm here to help you through
the tough days, the lonely nights,
the angry heart, the tears.
I'm here.

When you need the
warmth of a hug,
a hand to hold you steady,
the reassuring voice
of someone who cares.
I'm here.

I can't change the things that
brought you to this place in your life,
but I can help you work through it.
I can help you see that whatever
life brings your way,
you are stronger than you believe,
and that you don't have to face it alone.
I'm here.

Believe in yourself.
Know that you have the power
to get through this.
And if you should stumble
along the way,
If you need the strength of
a friend, just know
I'm here.

Heart, Be Still

A heart breaks and
the sadness seeps
out. Sadness rich
with pain and regret.
Sadness that knows the
path to the soul.

A heart breaks and
dreams die. Dreams
fuzzy with hopes that
fade away. Dreams
tainted with sadness
of the heart.

A broken heart,
still beating. Each
beat pulsing with
pain and broken dreams.
Please heart, be still.

A heart breaks and
loneliness paints the
day. Each day turns
into night, and each night
to tortured dreams
of once was.

A heart breaks and
the sadness seeps out.
Dreams die and loneliness
paints the day. A heart
breaks, yet still beats.

Please.
Heart.
Be still.

Just Another Day

Just another day.
Another day - watching
dreams once grand
scattered to the wind.

Bits and pieces float
through the air. Dreams
once vibrant, dreams once
close to the heart, caught
by the current of life…
drift, drift away.

I try to catch them.
Try to catch just one. Just
one to keep, but the current
is too strong.

Maybe I just stopped caring
enough to hold them close. I let
them go – and realized too late that
dreams could be so elusive.
That I just don't have the strength
to keep them close

Bits and pieces float
through the air. Caught by
the current of life…

Heartbeat

<hr>

You touched my heart.
You captured each beat,
and made it your own. Two
hearts beating as one. Two
hearts waiting to grow.

Heartbeat, please come
back to me.

Safe and warm, I gave my
heart away. Beat by beat.
Each beat making you
stronger with my love.
Each beat taking part of me.

Heartbeat, please come
back to me.

One heart wanting to beat
alone. Your heart, wanting to be free.
But still, you take each beat of my own.
Please, let my heartbeat free.

Heartbeat, please come
Back to me.

I gave my heart away, and now, your
heart beats…alone. I need to be
whole, I need to be free.
Just a heartbeat away.

Heartbeat.
Please.
Come back to me.

Goodbye My Hero

He talks to me, animated and happy, but I don't
hear his words. I focus on the breathing tube
in his nose, the IV drips, and the beep of the
monitoring devices in this sterile, lonely room.

I see the frail man before me with the prognosis of
death, and am overcome with the feeling of loss.
Where is the tough and sturdy man who molded me
into who I am today? Where is the who man who
can win at anything - the man who does not accept defeat?

I try. I try so hard not to cry, try not to accept
the fact that soon, he will be gone. The foundation
of my life will weaken. My hero will be defeated
by circumstances beyond his control. And yet,
he talks to me, animated and happy. He is
content with the knowledge that he is dying.

I try. I try not to cry - but the tears fall like stones
upon my cheeks. He sees yet says nothing. He
simply reaches for my hand. He sighs and smiles,
then speaks.

He tells me not to be sad. He tells me that I should
live with passion and love with abandon. That I should
live each day with joy, and that I should not be
afraid to love, or to lose at love as these things will
make me stronger. He tells me to take pride in the man
that I have become - and vow to grow better each day. He tells
me that he will be with me, every step of every day, that I
should not be sad that he is gone, but to find joy in the time
we have shared.

I smile through the tears and squeeze the hand of my hero.

My Dad.

About the Author

Larry L. Black, a cancer survivor, is an American poet and artist who currently resides in Durham, North Carolina. He served with honor in the U.S. military and has worked for the federal government in Germany, North Carolina, Virginia, Washington, D.C., and Florida.

His first book, The Fuzzy Color of Broken Dreams, published in 2011, was recently republished under the title "Whispers from the Heart".

www.ingramcontent.com/pod-product-compliance
Lightning Source LLC
Chambersburg PA
CBHW051817050726
47598CB00006B/2603